#RADIOLOG

A SNARKY COLORING BOOK FOR ADULTS

MW00352476

Want free goodies?
Email us at freebies@pbleu.com

@papeteriebleu

Papeterie Bleu

Shop our other books at
www.pbleu.com

Wholesale distribution through Ingram Content Group
www.ingramcontent.com/publishers/distribution/wholesale

For questions and customer service, email us at
support@pbleu.com

© Papeterie Bleu. All rights reserved. No part of this publication may be reproduced, distributed, or transmitted, in any form or by any means, including photocopying, recording, or other electronic or mechanical methods, without prior written permission of the publisher, except in the case of brief quotations embodied in critical reviews and certain other noncommercial uses permitted by copyright law.

FREE PDF DOWNLOAD OF THIS BOOK

RESISTANCE
IS NOT FUTILE
(IT'S VOLTAGE DIVIDED BY
IN A MOMENT, YOU WILL TASTE METAL AND WET YOURSELF
IT'S GOING TIBIA OK

www.pbleu.com/radiology

YOUR DOWNLOAD CODE: RAD373

@papeteriebleu

Papeterie Bleu

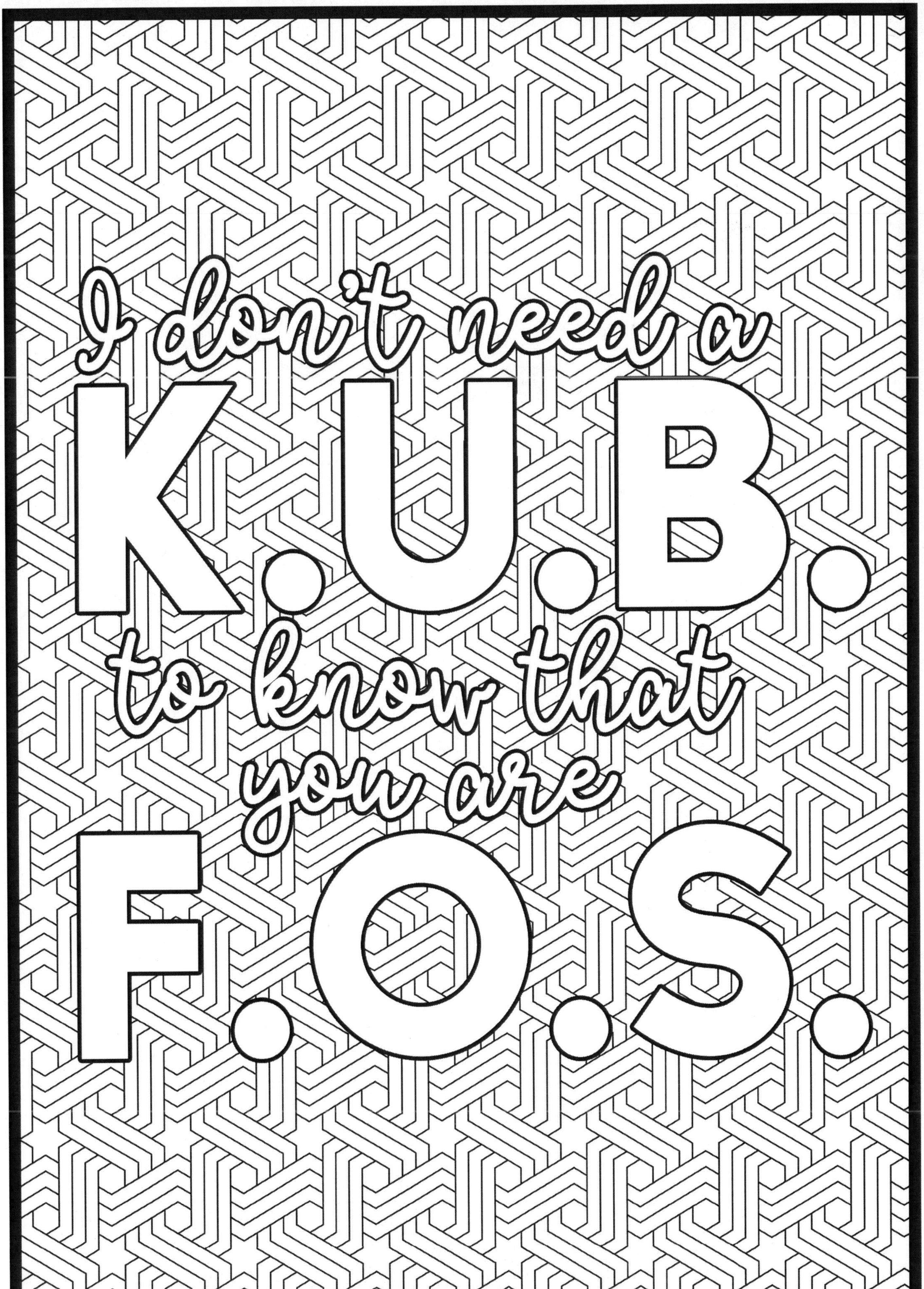
I don't need a
K.U.B.
to know that
you are
F.O.S.

SORRY YOU'RE HURT,
BUT MOMMY'S IN
Radiology
AND WE ONLY
GO TO THE
ER IF I THINK IT'S
BROKEN
XRAY

RESISTANCE
IS NOT FUTILE!
(IT'S VOLTAGE DIVIDED BY CURRENT)

36.6

I'D AGREE
with you
BUT THEN
WE'D BOTH
be wrong

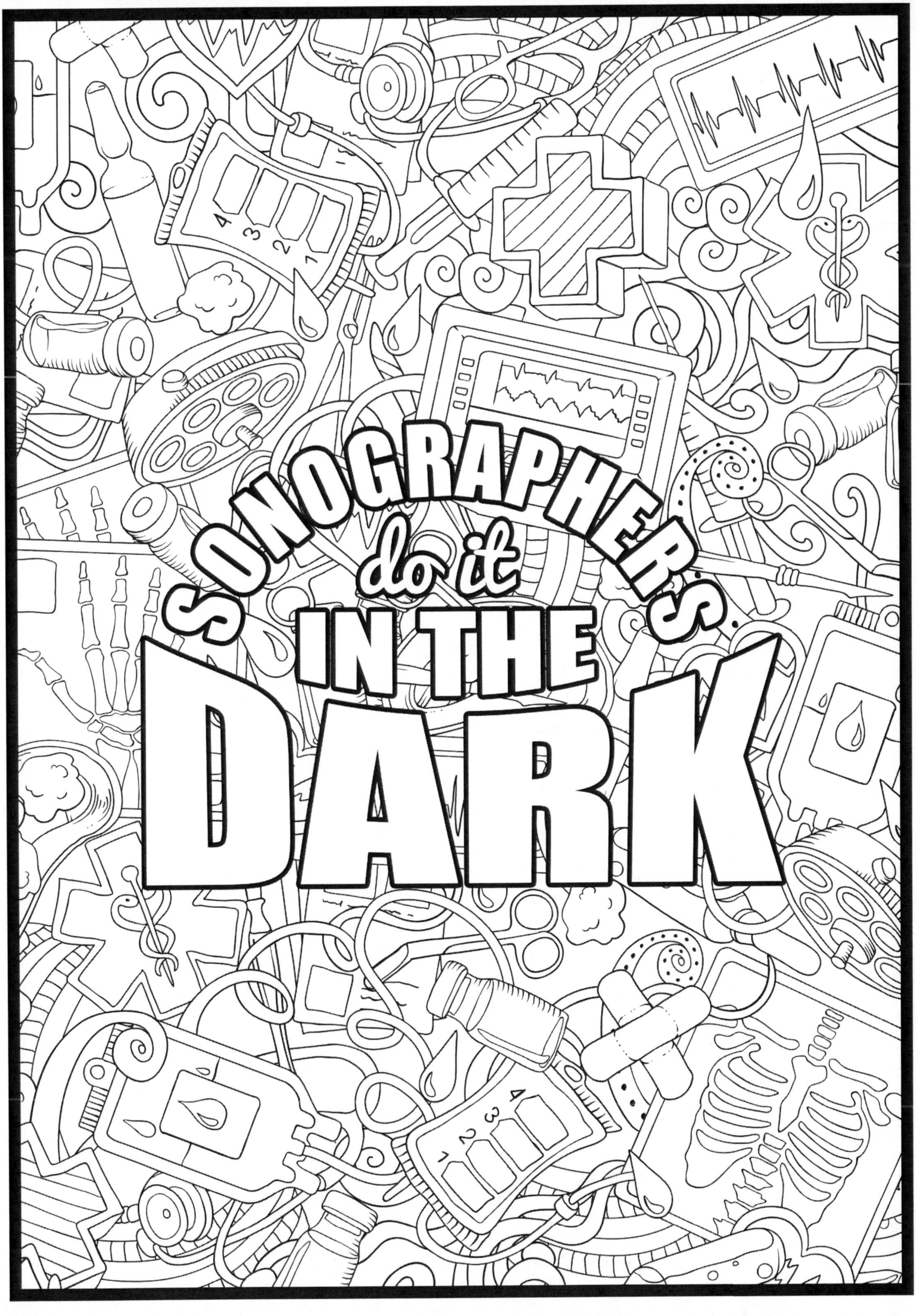
SONOGRAPHERS
do it
IN THE
DARK

I LOST MY X-ray marker...
THE REST OF MY DAY IS NOW CRAP!

IT'S GOING
TIBIA
OK

I'M WAY
TOO
Sick
FOR WORK
BUT SHOULD
BE FINE FOR
Happy
Hour
PUB
BEER
PUB
Best beer here

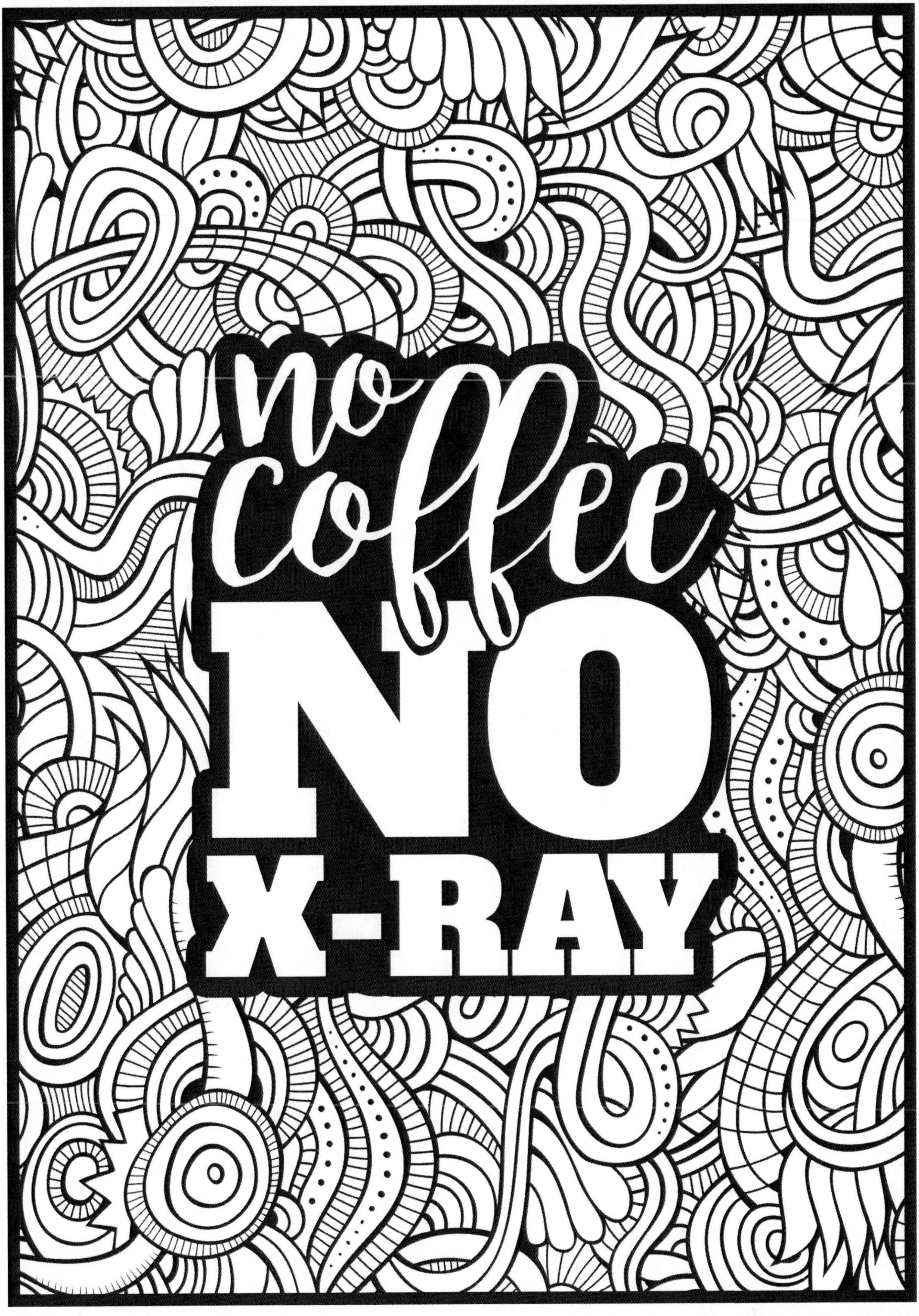
no coffee
NO
X-RAY

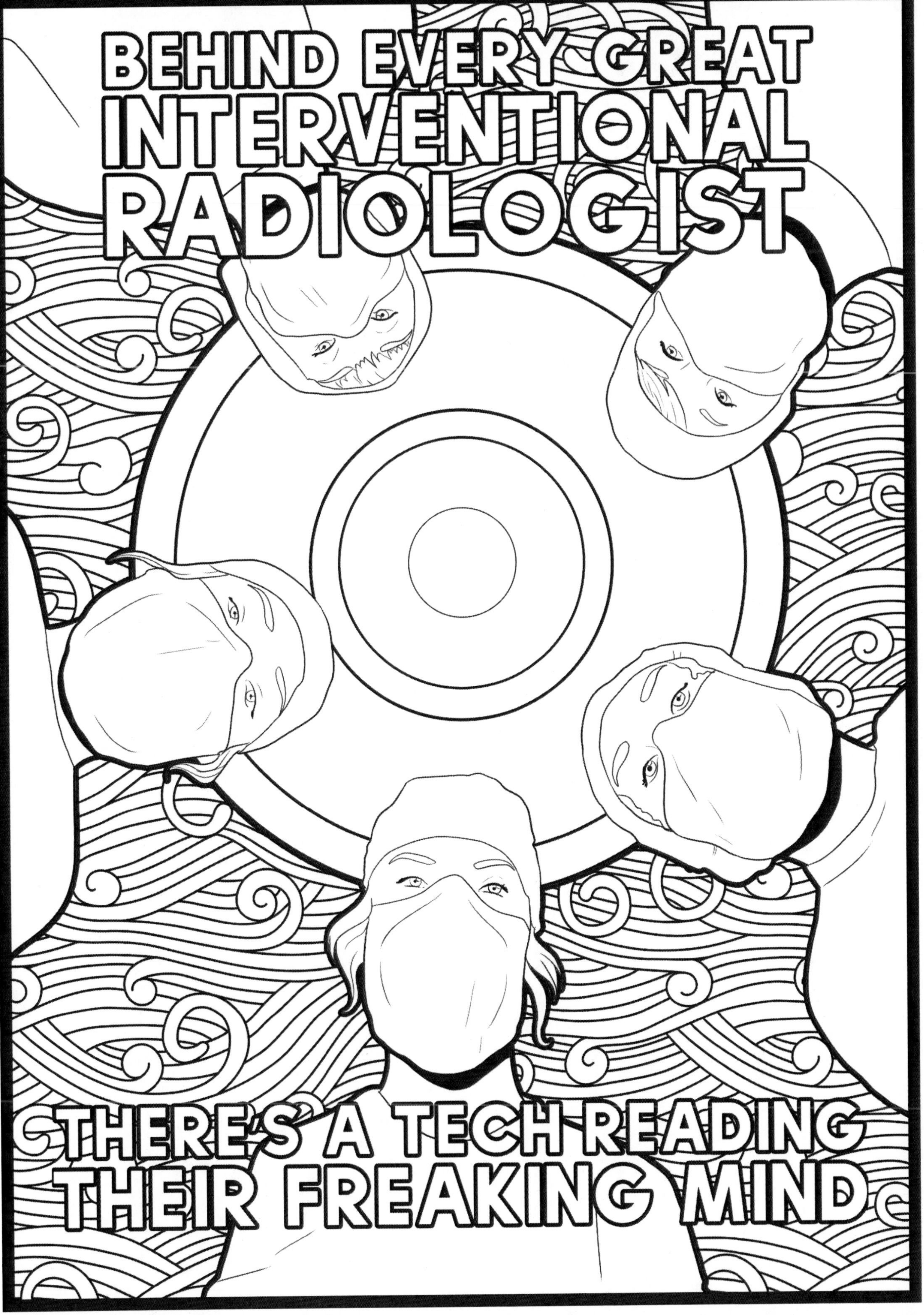
BEHIND EVERY GREAT
INTERVENTIONAL
RADIOLOGIST
THERE'S A TECH READING
THEIR FREAKING MIND

DON'T HATE,
RADIATE
250ml

KEEP
CALM
and
X-RAY
ON

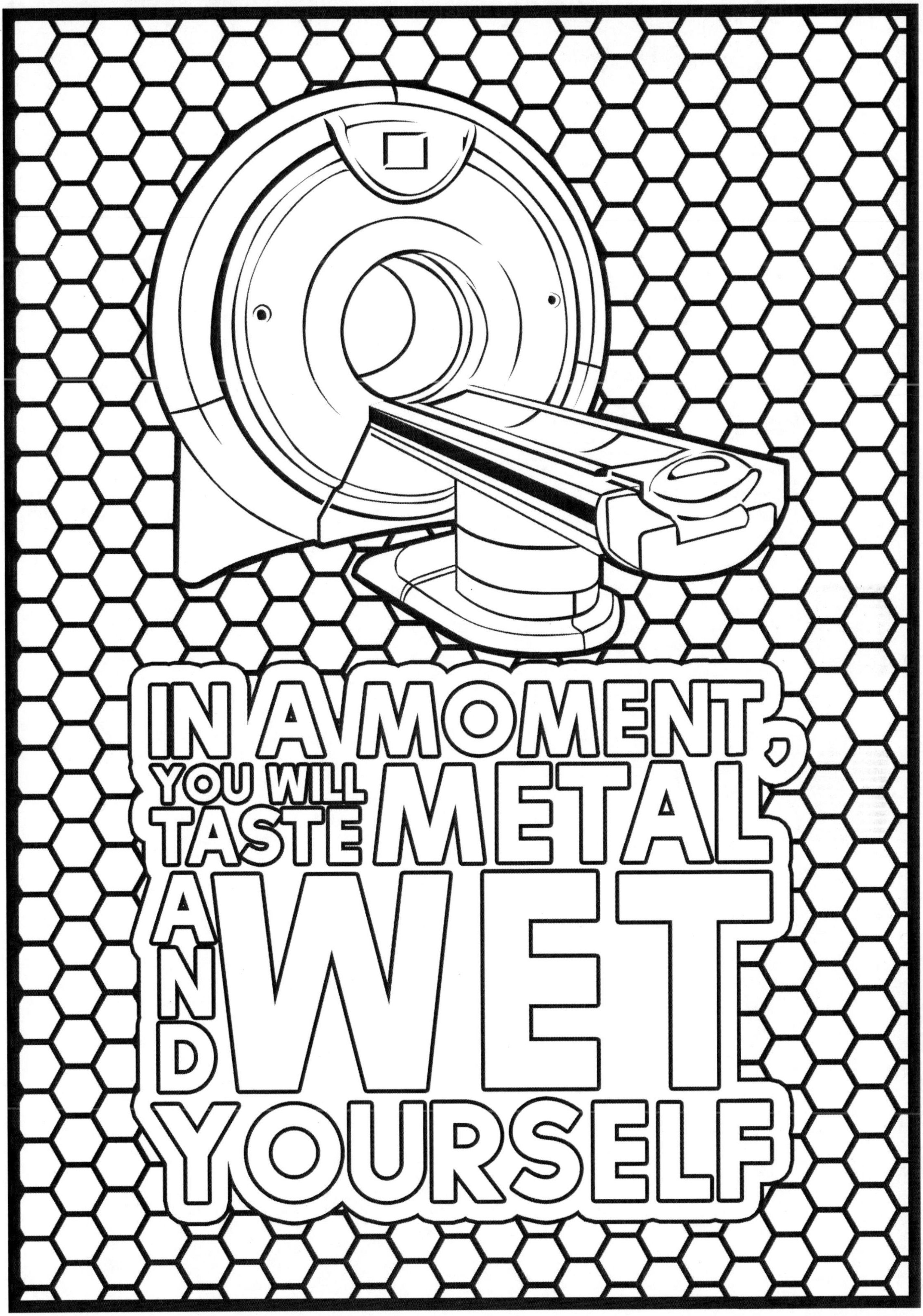
IN A MOMENT,
YOU WILL TASTE METAL
AND WET
YOURSELF

you must be a
PHOTON,
BECAUSE YOU JUST
TOOK ME TO MY
EXCITED
STATE

HOSPITAL
HOSPITAL

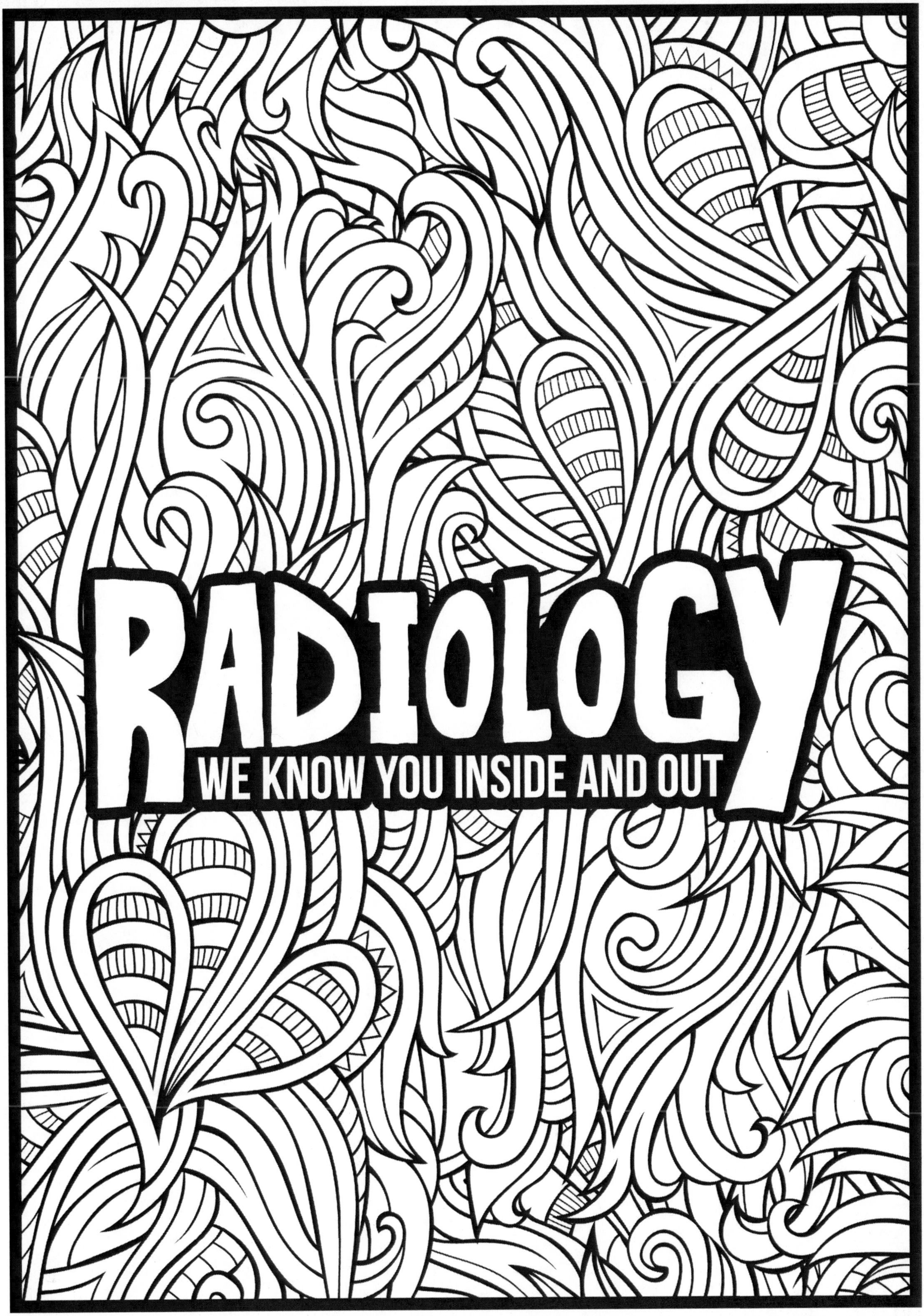
RADIOLOGY
WE KNOW YOU INSIDE AND OUT

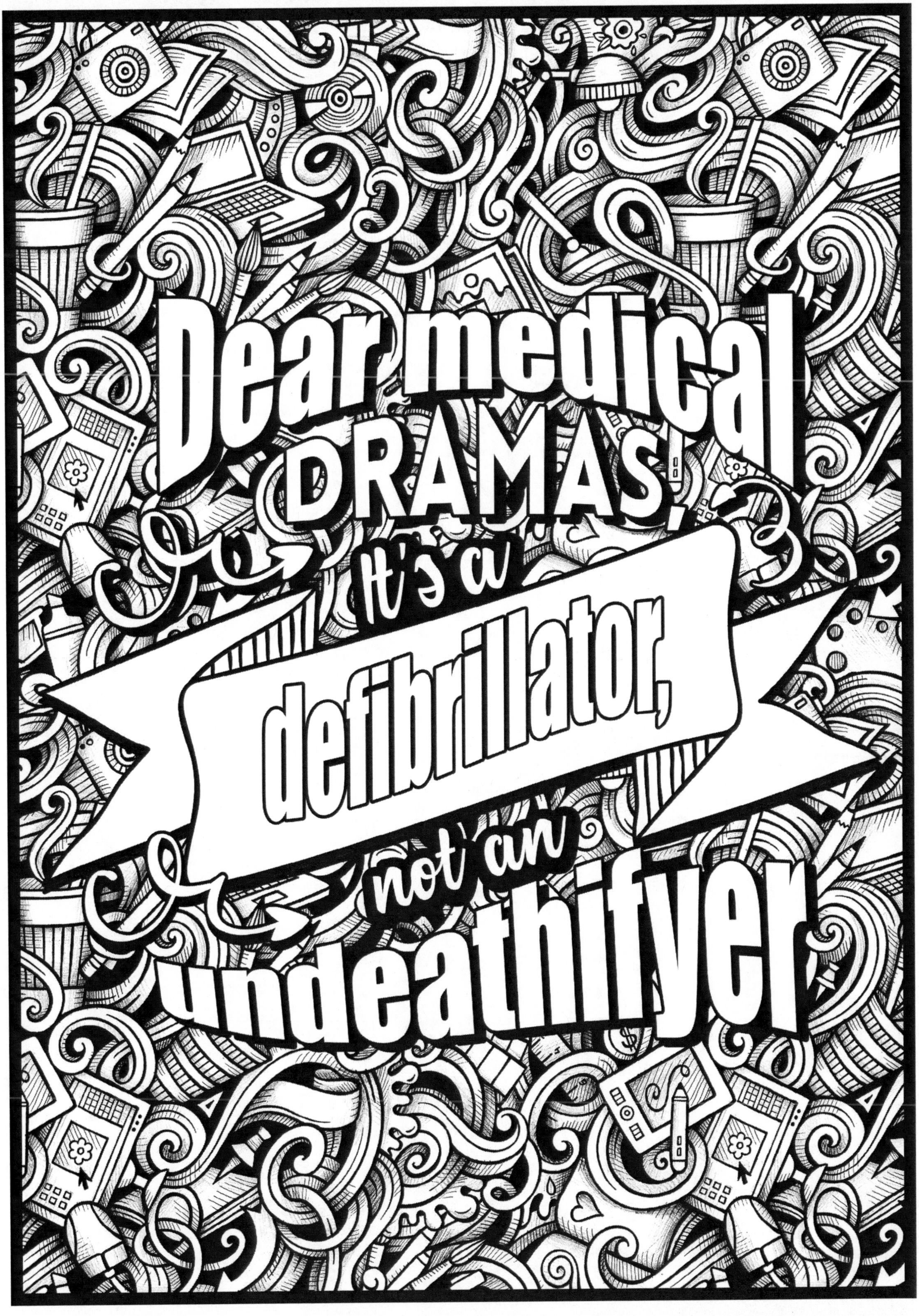
Dear medical
DRAMAS,
It's a
defibrillator,
not an
undeathifyer

BARIUM
BARISTA

XRAY
LIFE

36.6

IF YOU FIB
HR 80
Selected
4:30:04
SpO2 99
99
SpO2
I WILL PADDLE YOU

YOU don't have to be CRAZY to work here
WE'LL TRAIN YOU.

NOT ALL PATIENTS ARE
annoying
SOME ARE
unconscious

JOHNNY HAS 12 CANDY BARS. HE EATS 10.
What does he have now?
DIABETES.
JOHNNY
has
DIABETES.

HOSPITAL

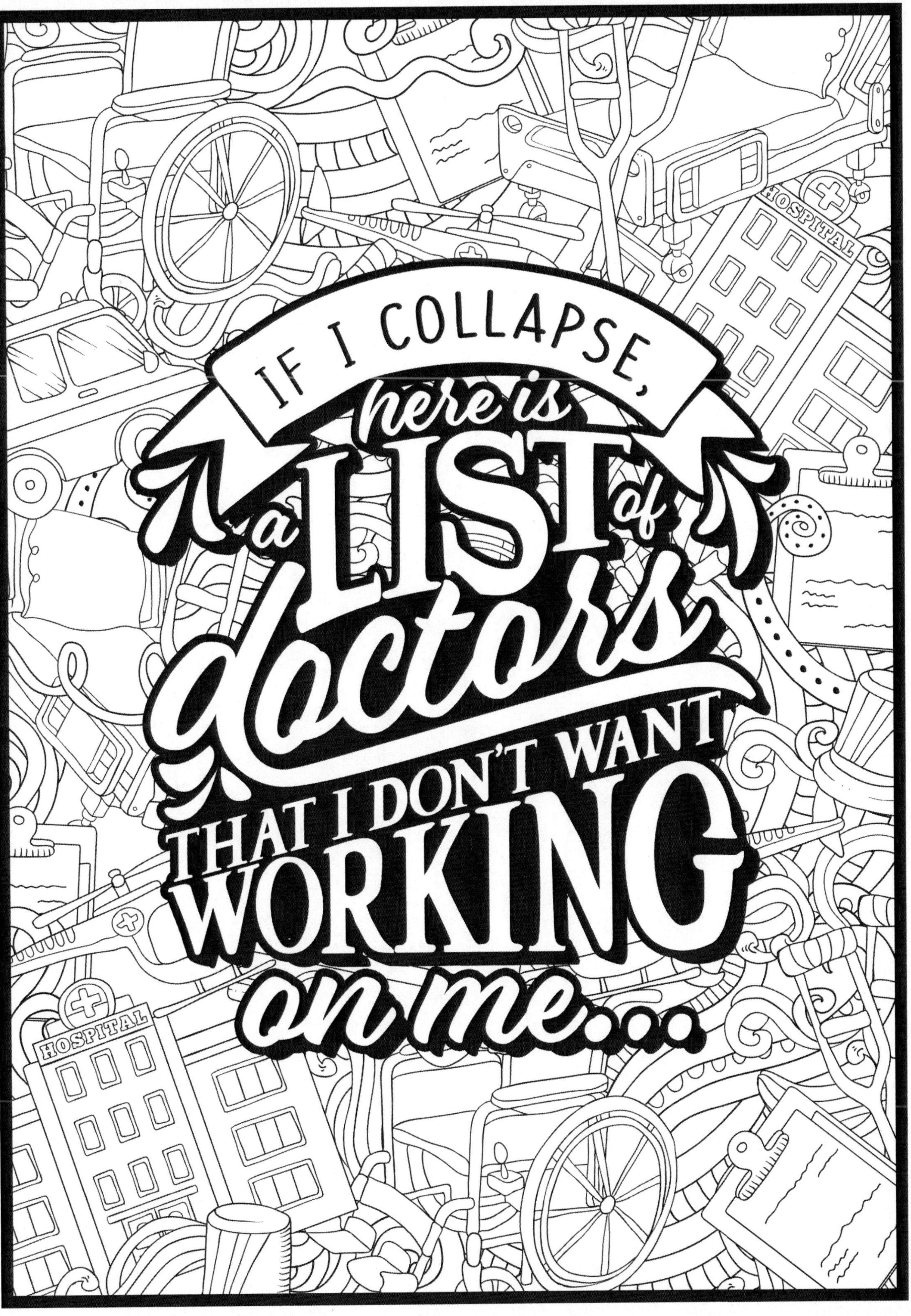
IF I COLLAPSE,
here is
a LIST of
doctors
THAT I DON'T WANT
WORKING
on me...
HOSPITAL
HOSPITAL

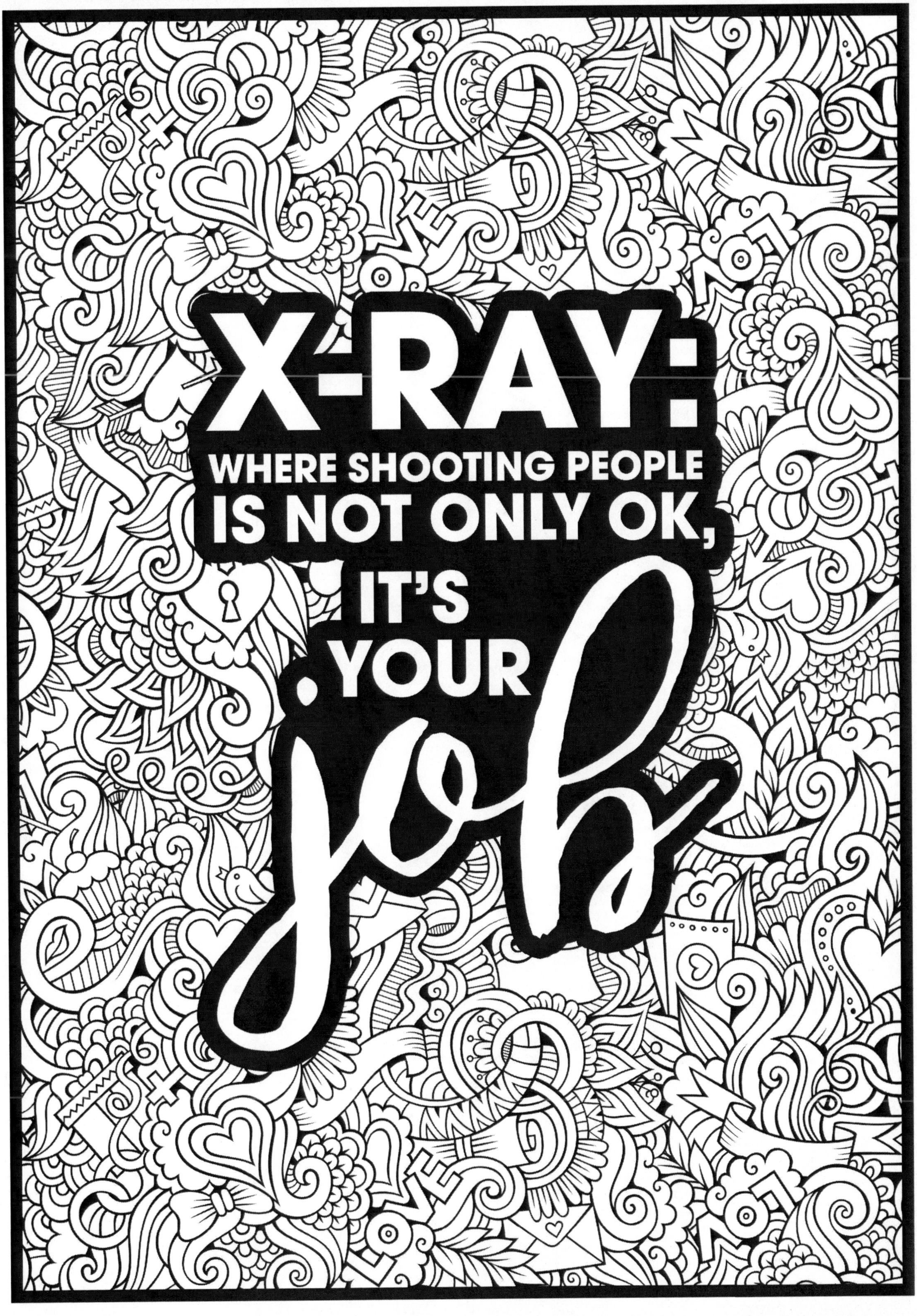
X-RAY:
WHERE SHOOTING PEOPLE
IS NOT ONLY OK,
IT'S
YOUR
job

KEEP
CALM
OR I WILL
CALL
ANESTHESIA

HOSPITAL

#thestruggleisreal
WHAT TO WEAR... WHAT TO WEAR...
#SCRUBLIFE

all bleeding
Stops
EVENTUALLY

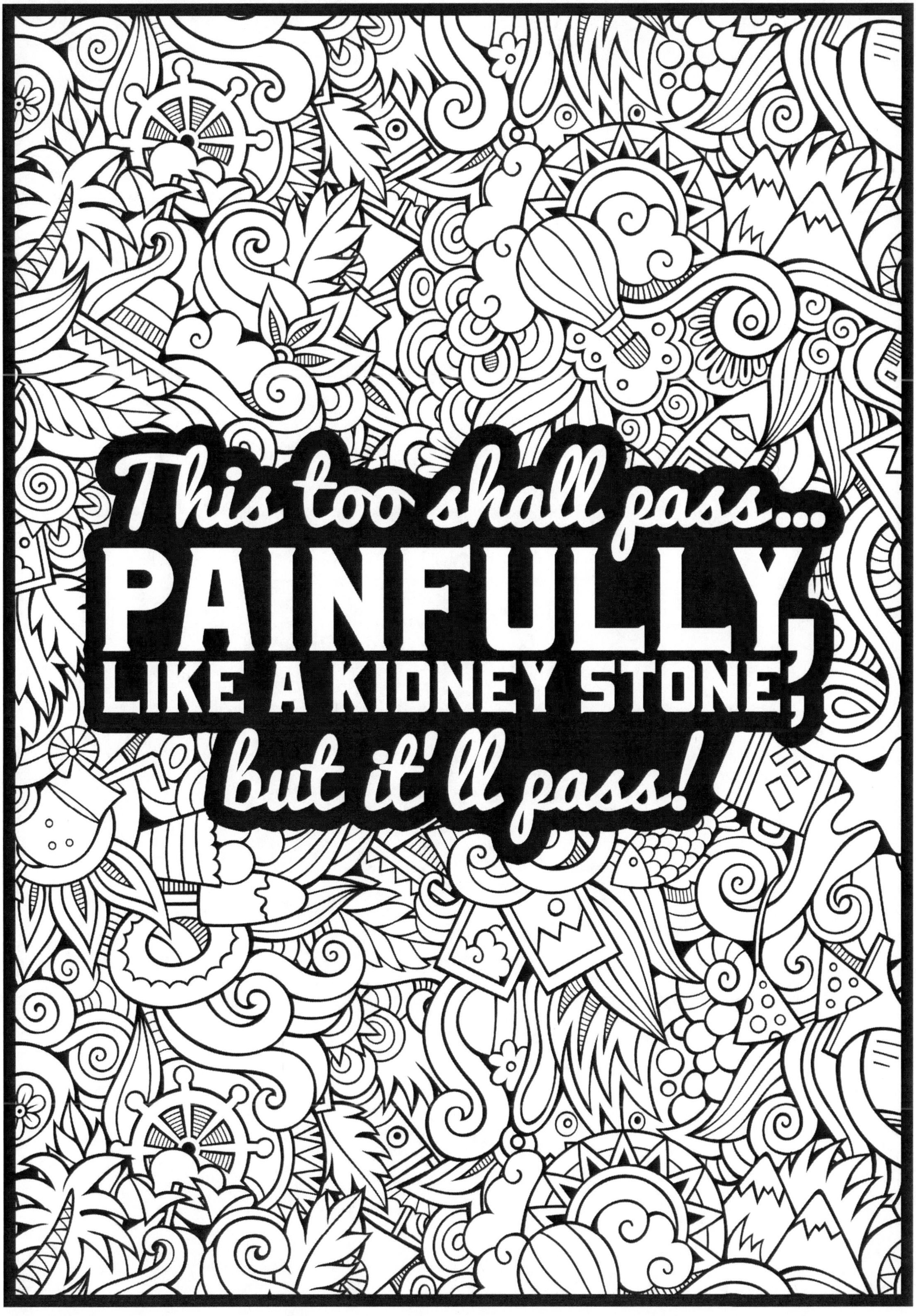
This too shall pass...
PAINFULLY,
LIKE A KIDNEY STONE,
but it'll pass!

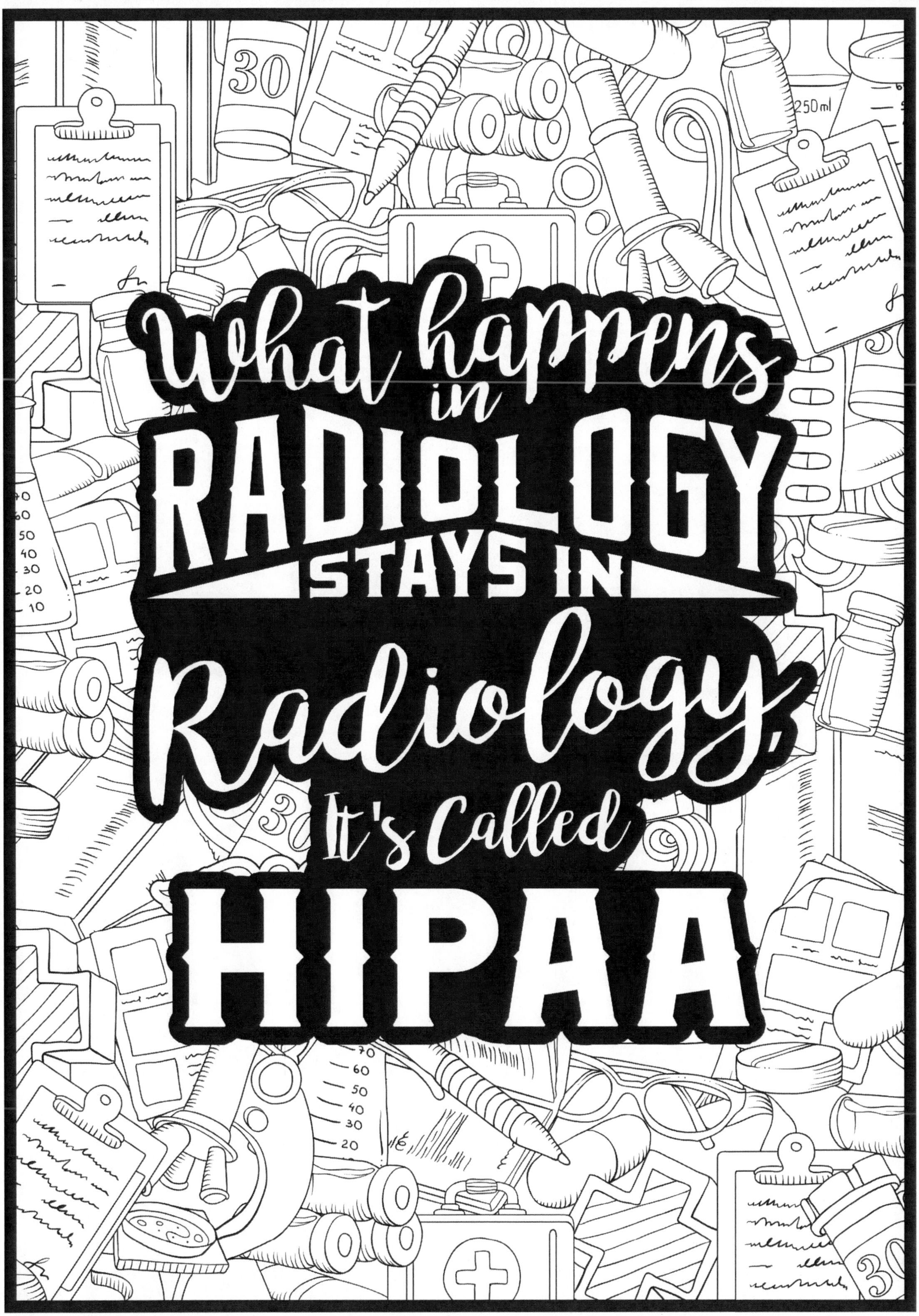
What happens
in
RADIOLOGY
STAYS IN
Radiology,
It's Called
HIPAA

WHEN I GET OFF THE PHONE WITH YOU, I'M GOING TO TELL MY CO-WORKERS HOW STUPID YOU ARE.

WARNING
TO AVOID SERIOUS INJURY
DON'T TELL ME HOW
TO DO MY JOB

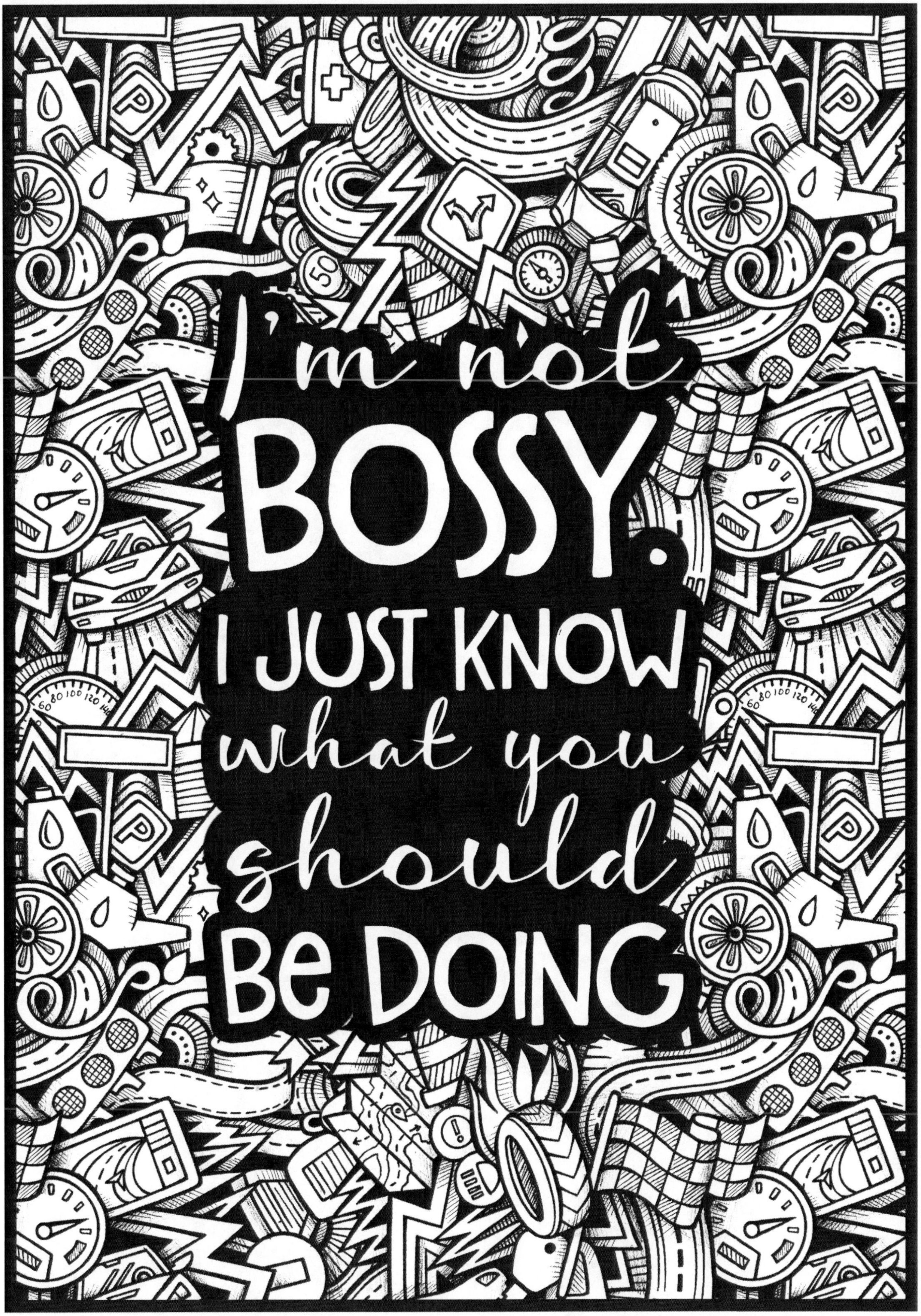
I'm not
BOSSY.
I JUST KNOW
what you
should
Be DOING

That moment
WHEN YOU HAVE TO
pee
REALLY BAD
BUT YOU CAN'T
GET THE DRAWSTRING
of your scrubs
UNTIED

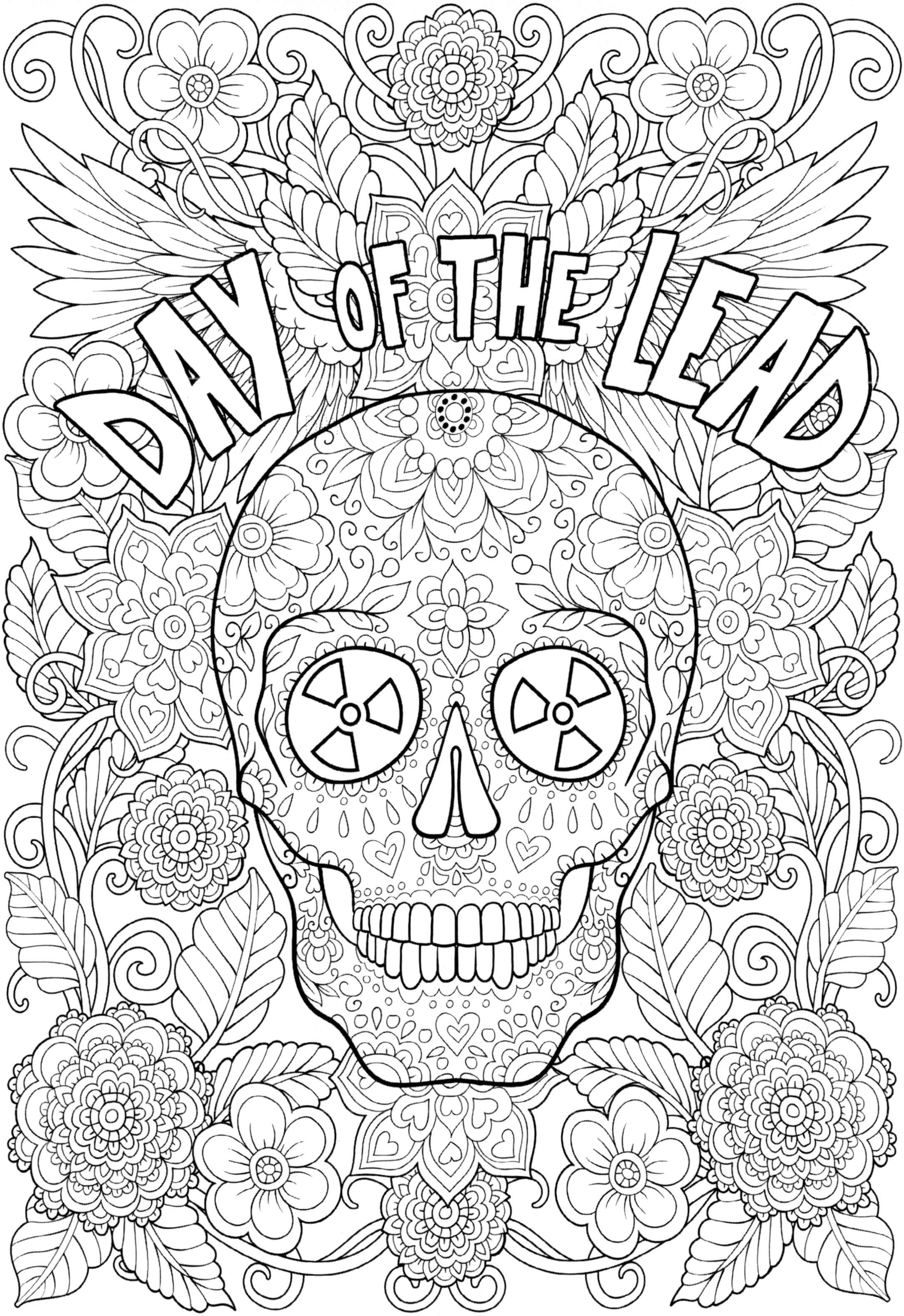
DAY OF THE LEAD

I DON'T
always
WATCH
MEDICAL SHOWS,
but when I do,
I POINT OUT
EVERY
SINGLE
MEDICAL
INACCURACY

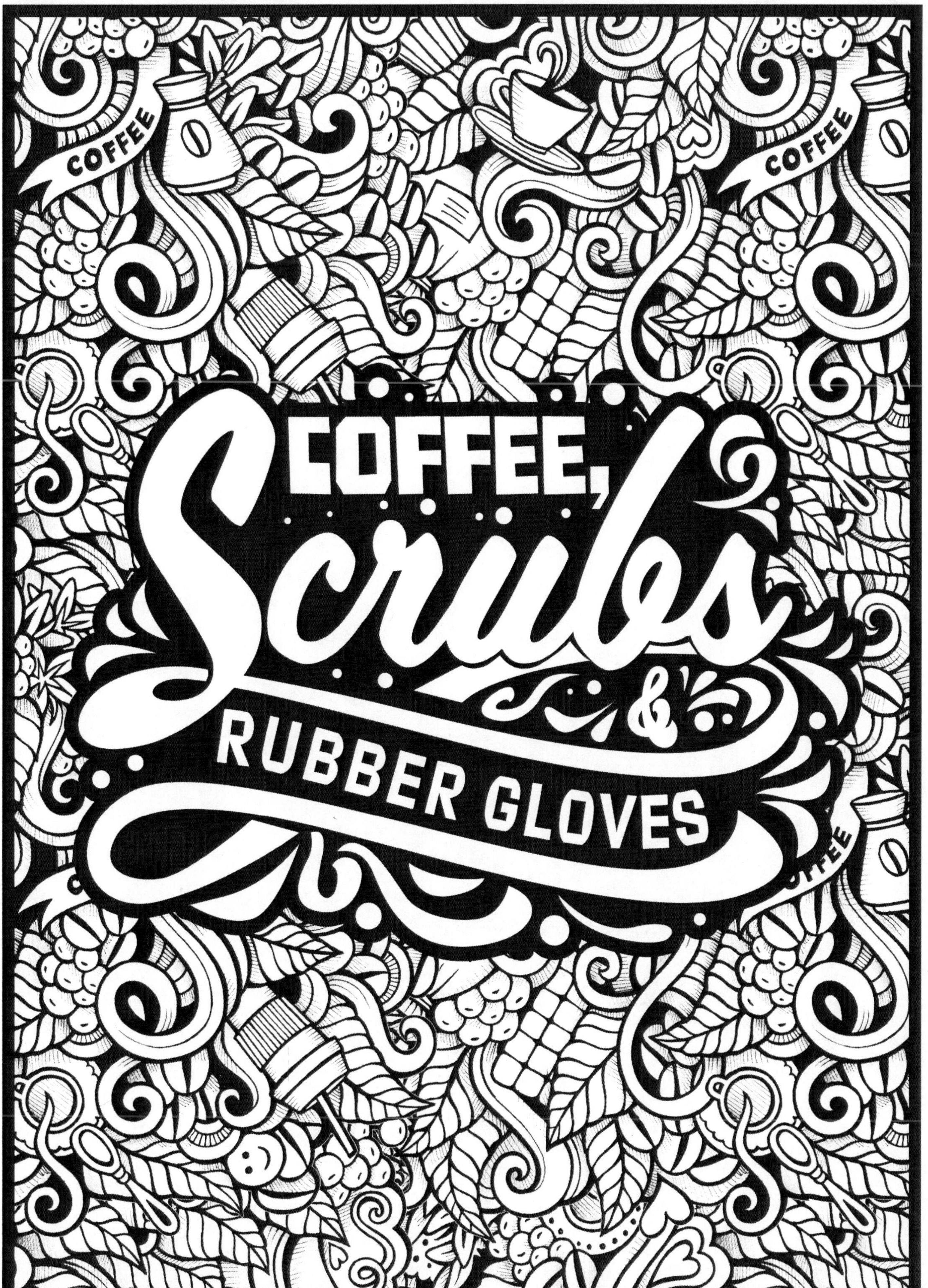
COFFEE,
Scrubs
&
RUBBER GLOVES
COFFEE
COFFEE

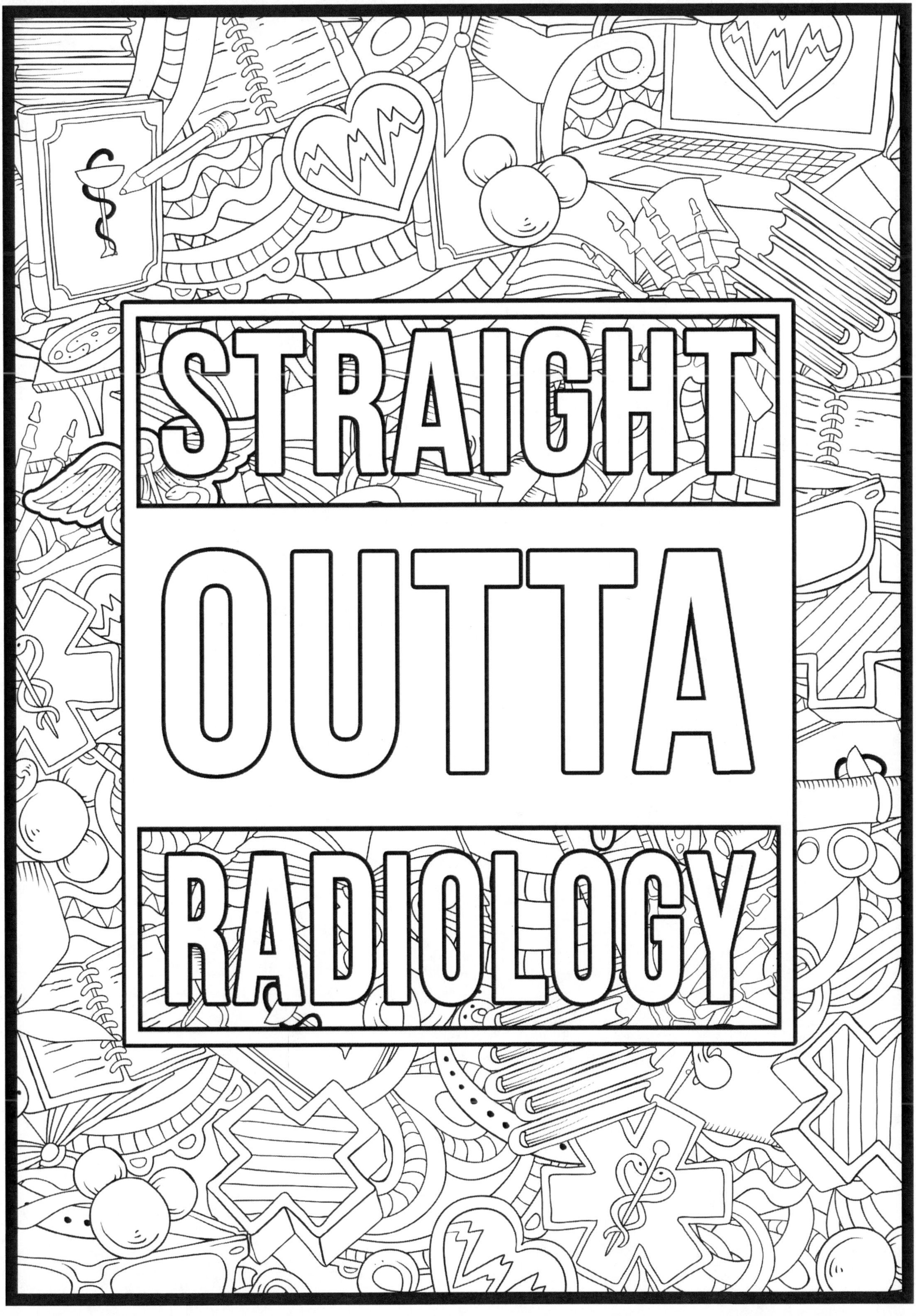
STRAIGHT
OUTTA
RADIOLOGY

HEY, I JUST MET YOU,
AND
YOU SEEM
crazy,
SO
HERE'S SOME
HALDOL,
AND
ATIVAN,
MAYBE.

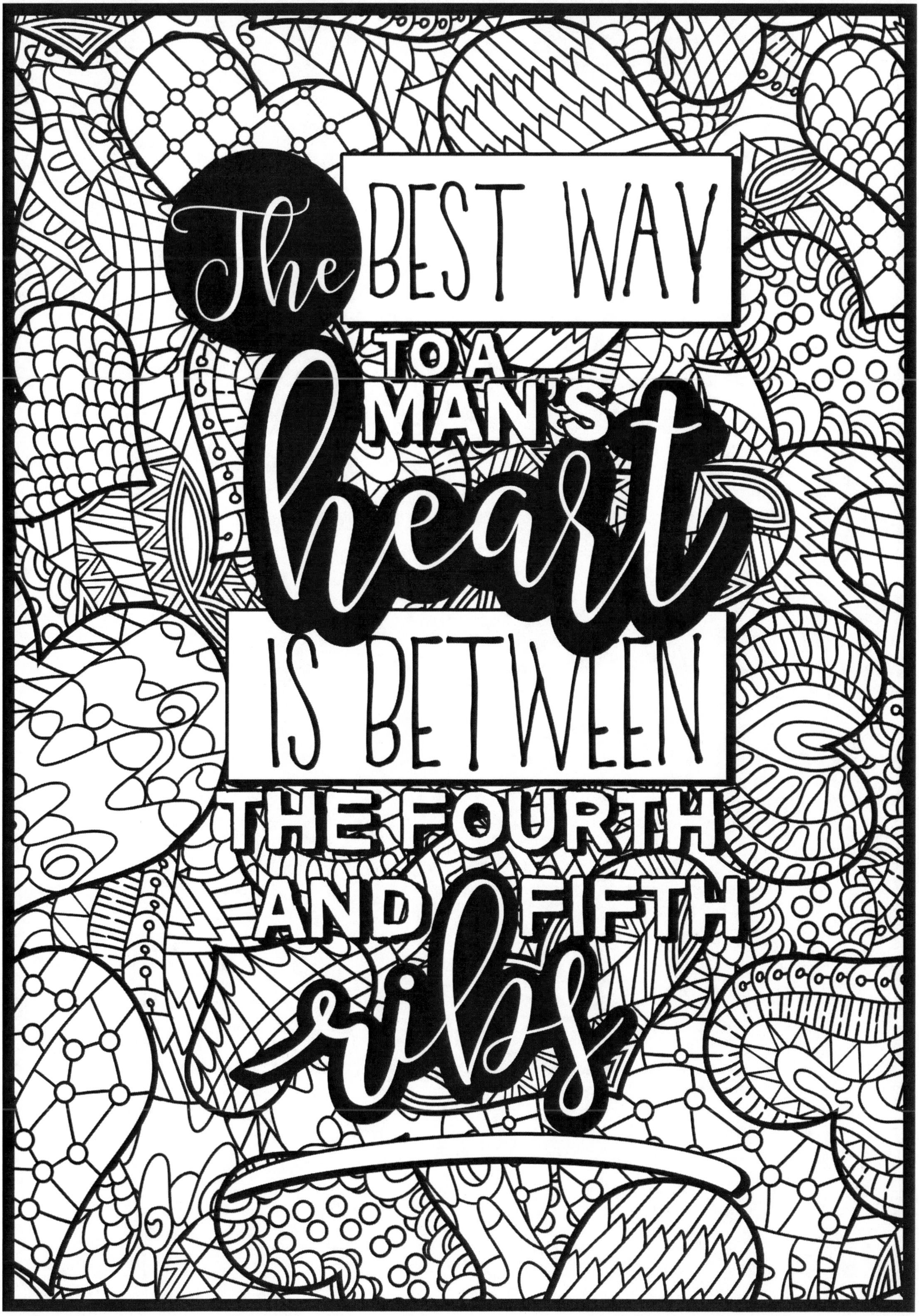
The BEST WAY
TO A
MAN'S
heart
IS BETWEEN
THE FOURTH
AND FIFTH
ribs

I'M CURRENTLY
EXPERIENCING
life
at
the
SPEED
of 15 WTFs
Per Hour

HOSPITAL

DEATH
BEFORE
DECAF

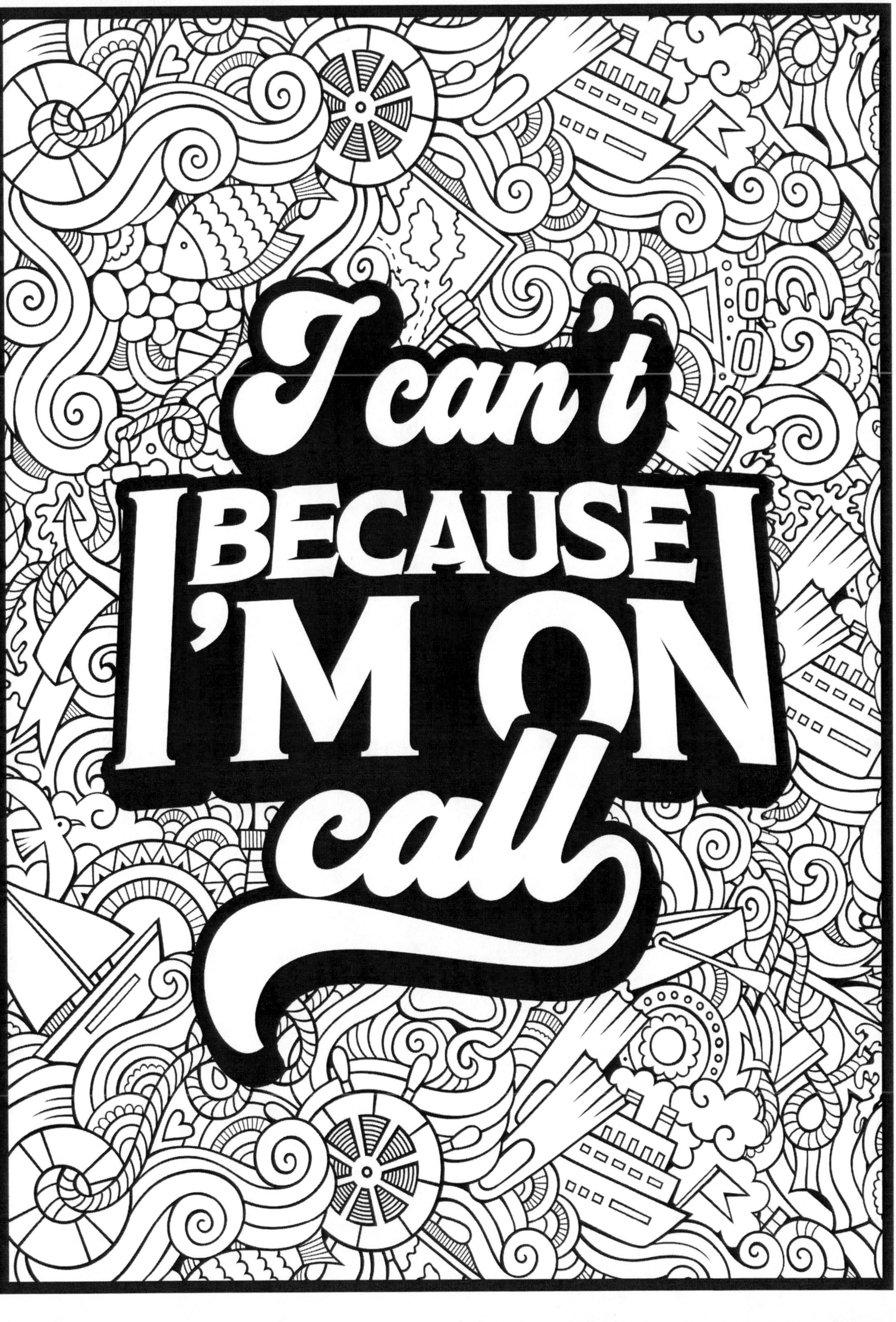
I can't
BECAUSE
I'M ON
call

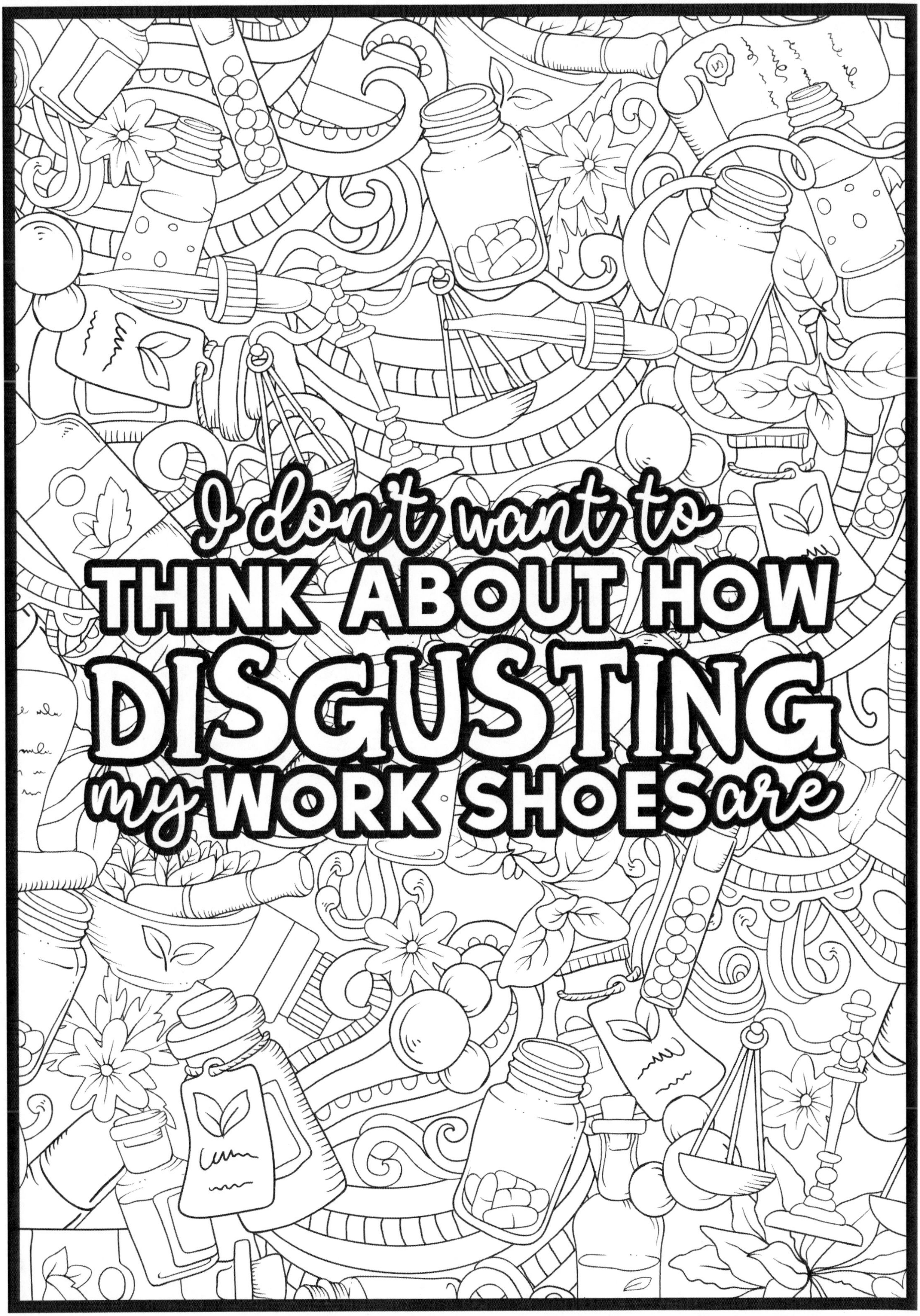
I don't want to
THINK ABOUT HOW
DISGUSTING
my WORK SHOES are

Dear God,
please let my
patients be
Skinny
tomorrow.
Amen.

I don't have
A PROBLEM
with
caffeine.
I have a problem
without
CAFFEINE.

I already
WANT to
TAKE A NAP
TOMORROW

I need a
HUG.....E
bottle
of WINE
Wine
Wine
Wine
Wine

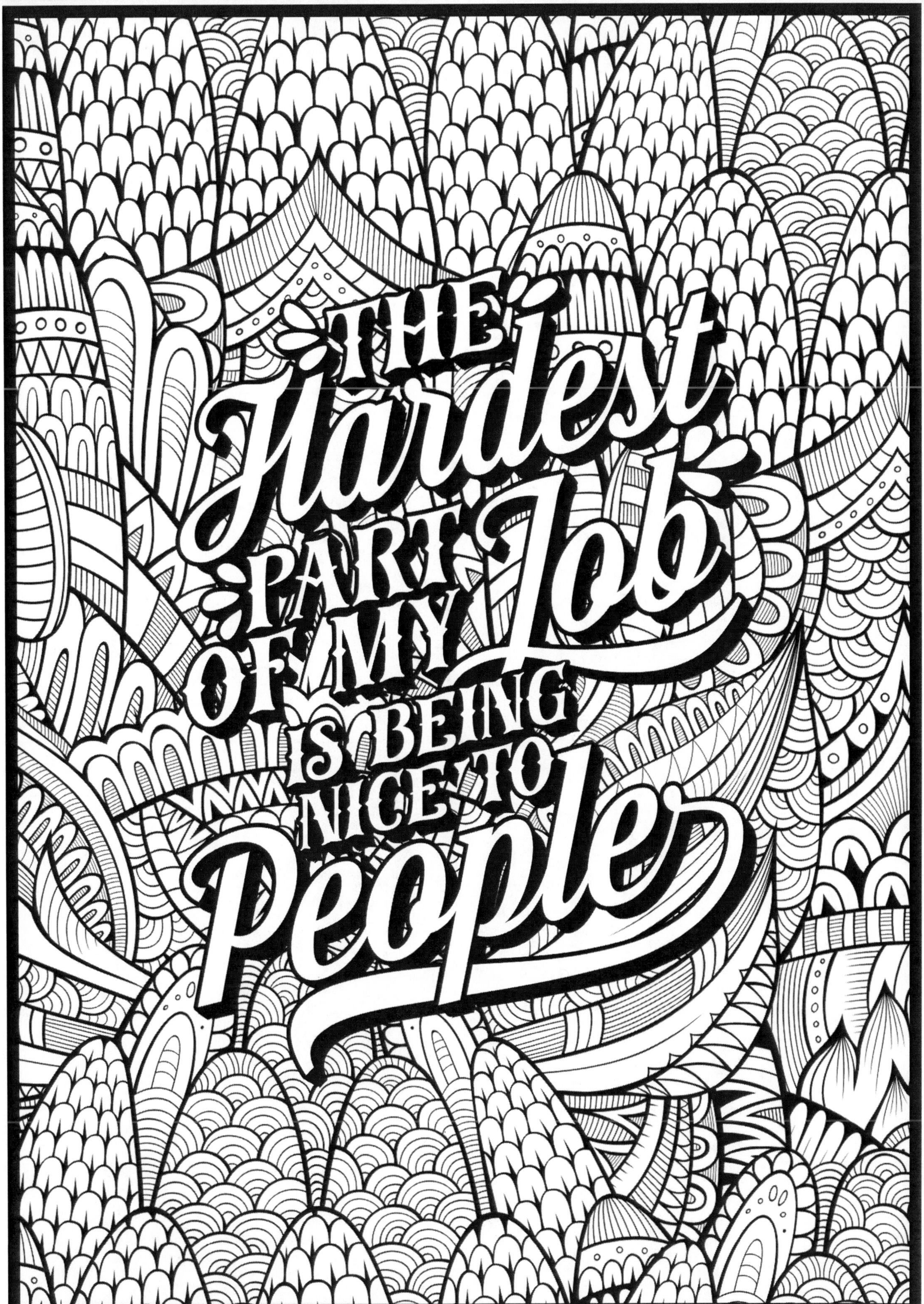
THE
Hardest
PART
OF MY
Job
IS BEING
NICE TO
People

Actually
MEDICINE
IS THE BEST
MEDICINE
36.6

HOSPITAL
HOSPITAL

LIVIN' THE
SCRUB
LIFE

oh snap!

FREE PDF DOWNLOAD OF THIS BOOK

RESISTANCE
IS NOT FUTILE
(IT'S VOLTAGE DIVIDED BY CURRENT
IN A MOMENT,
YOU WILL TASTE METAL
AND WET
YOURSELF
IT'S GOING
TIBIA
OK

www.pbleu.com/radiology

YOUR DOWNLOAD CODE: RAD373

@papeteriebleu

Papeterie Bleu

Want free goodies?
Email us at freebies@pbleu.com

@papeteriebleu

Papeterie Bleu

Shop our other books at
www.pbleu.com

Wholesale distribution through Ingram Content Group
www.ingramcontent.com/publishers/distribution/wholesale

For questions and customer service, email us at
support@pbleu.com

Made in United States
North Haven, CT
09 December 2022

28254966R10061